THE ART OF METAL & WIRE

JANET WILSON

SEARCH PRESS

First published in Great Britain 2003
Search Press Limited
Wellwood
North Farm Road
Tunbridge Wells
Kent TN2 3DR

Originally published in The Netherlands 2002 by
Uitgeverij Cantecleer
Postbus 309
3740 AH Baarn
The Netherlands
Cantecleer is part of Tirion Publisher bv

Original title:
Stijlvol metaalfolie: metaalfolie, metaaldraad en gaas

Copyright © 2002 Tirion Uitgevers bv, Baarn
Patterns and diagrams copyright © 2002 Janet Wilson

Cover: Hans Britsemmer, Kudelstaart
DTP: Cees Overoorde, Utrecht
Photography: Hennie Raaymakers, St Michielsgestel
Photography Styling: Willemien Mommersteeg,
St Michielsgestel

English translation by Janet Wilson
English translation copyright © Search Press Limited 2003

ISBN 1 903975 93 X

Suppliers

If you have difficulty in obtaining any of the materials and
equipment mentioned in this book, then please visit the
Search Press website for details of suppliers:
www.searchpress.com

Alternatively, you can write to the Publishers at the address
above, for a current list of stockists, including firms which
operate a mail-order service.

The author would like to thank the following companies for
their help and co-operation:

Starform – The Netherlands
Delta Technical Coatings Inc. – USA
Amaco Europe Ltd. – England and USA
Dreamweaver Stencils – USA
Whichcraft of Broomhill – England
Kars & Co. – The Netherlands
Harvey Baker Design – England
Artistic Wire – USA
Bond™ – America
Lazertran – England and USA
The Stamp Connection – England
Hero Arts Rubber Stamp Inc. – USA
Stampendous Inc. – USA
Xyron UK Ltd. – England and Germany
Fiskars – USA
OPITEC Hobbyfix – England and Germany
Ranger Industries Inc. – USA

Photograph on page 29 by kind courtesy of Royal Talens,
Apeldoorn, The Netherlands

Copying instruction

Many of the patterns in this book have had to be reduced –
some must be enlarged to 141%, others to 200%. 141% is
the standard enlargement for paper sizes A4 to A3 and most
photocopiers will have this setting. Some machines do not
have the facility for 200% enlargements, but if you enlarge
the pattern to 141% then enlarge the copy to 141% again,
the second copy will be almost 200%.

Note on conversions

The author refers to metric measurements throughout this
book. To convert a measurement given in centimetres (cm)
to inches (in) multiply by 0.3937. Some useful conversions
are listed below:

Metric to imperial	
1mm	0.04in
2mm	0.08in
3mm	0.12in
4mm	0.16in
5mm	0.20in
1cm	0.39in
2cm	0.79in
5cm	1.97in
10cm	3.94in
15cm	5.91in
20cm	7.87in
25cm	9.84in
30cm	11.81in
35cm	13.78in

CONTENTS

FOREWORD

Metal and wire are among my favourite mediums and it is a joy to have this opportunity to write a book about them and show you some of the ways that I have enjoyed combining and using them over the years.

We all need to nourish our creativity and I would like to thank two of my talented designer colleagues for feeding mine! Erica Fortgens allowed me to adapt some of her early paper embroidery designs to wire embroidery and Jana Ewy gave me the idea of making neck purses. My heartfelt thanks to both of you and I hope that you both take inspiration from the way I have used your ideas.

I would like to thank the many readers of my books over the years for the kind and generous comments they have made and I hope that this book will further your enjoyment and help you expand your creativity.

Have fun and many happy creative hours.

Janet Wilson

GENERAL INSTRUCTIONS

Tools

- pliers: needle-nosed, bent-nosed and nylon-jaw, flat-nosed
- side cutters
- wire jig
- wire winder and selection of mandrels
- insulated tweezers and regular tweezers with pointed ends
- nylon-headed hammer, club hammer (or small anvil) and a medium to heavyweight hammer
- texturing mallet. Make your own from a wooden or rubber mallet and a hot-glue gun (see page 7) or use a wooden meat tenderiser
- hand drill, and plastic-coated cup hook
- clutch pencil and modellers' miniature drill bits
- sewing needle
- large needle tool and perforating mat
- selection of paper embossing tools, an embossing wheel that runs easily along the edge of a ruler, brass embossing stencils, artists' paper stumps and a high-density foam embossing mat
- lino roller (block printer roller or a brayer)
- paper scissors, heavy-duty scissors and Fiskars decorative paper edgers
- scalpel, heavy-duty craft knife, steel-edged ruler and cutting mat
- Fiskars hand punches (a power punch machine could prove useful)
- fine round file
- rubber stamps and permanent dye ink stamp pads
- heat-proof, embossing craft sheet (or non-stick metal baking sheet) and a heat gun
- 3mm bamboo (or wooden) knitting needles
- four-pin French knitting bobbin and crochet hook

Materials

- metal sheet, various colours
- Art Emboss lightweight aluminium
- Wireform 6mm diamond mesh
- wire mesh in copper and brass
- coloured and silver wire – 12, 19, 23, 27, 30 and 33SWG
- eye pins, head pins, jump rings; silver eyelets and eyelet setting tool
- linen (or bookbinders' shirting)
- bookbinders' glue
- fine metallic thread, needles and pins
- normal and low-tack sticky tape
- double-sided sticky tape
- masking tape
- high-tack glue (Aleene's Designer Thick Tacky Glue) and a cocktail stick
- decorative craft stickers
- 7cm silver coloured purse frame with chain
- Lazertrans or Decal it
- selection of beads, charms and spacers, bead stringing wire, a gold coloured bolt fastener and a brooch pin
- a selection of cords/wool for making tassels
- picture frames – large MDF frame and medium and small nature paper photo frames and a selection of boxes
- flat-backed push mould polymer-clay head
- Brush 'n' Leaf (gold leaf) and brush
- Self-adhesive metal tape (Foil-it metal tape)
- Friendly Plastic
- Delta Paint Jewels
- Paris binding and black velvet ribbon
- tracing paper (90gsm)
- relief gloss lacquer
- memo block and spring clips
- selection of cards and papers colours of card, including Lace and hologram card
- greyboard, mount board or thick card
- permanent marker
- self-adhesive, hook and loop Velcro
- paper serviette and collage adhesive
- wooden dowel

Wire gauges

Wire is measured by gauge, standard wire gauge (SWG) or American wire gauge (AWG) or diameter (millimetre). SWG has been used in this book, but I have included the conversion table below to show the equivalents in AWG and millimetres.

SWG	AWG	Millimeters
42	38	0.10
33	30	0.25
30	28	0.32
27	26	0.40
25	24	0.50
23	22	0.63
22	21	0.71
20	19	0.90
19	18	1.00
18	16	1.25
12	10	2.00

BASIC TECHNIQUES

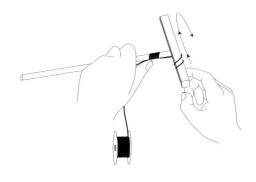

Using a wire winder

Although there are several types of wire winder available, most are T-shaped tools with a mandrel (shape former) as the uptight and a handle as the cross piece. A basic winder has a round mandrel, but you can also buy them with square or rectangular mandrels. If you a need large diameter winding or another shape – say a triangle – you can make your own from a length of balsa wood, wooden dowel or moulding.

Use 27SWG wire on a 3mm diameter mandrel for card borders. Use 23SWG wire on a 5 or 6mm diameter, or a 10 x 2mm rectangular mandrel for boxes and jewellery necklets.

The basic method of operation is to attach the wire to the handle, then rotate the handle to wind the wire on to the mandrel. First, wind a couple of turns of wire round the handle to secure it (some winders have a hole in the handle to help secure the wire). Next, lightly grip the mandrel with the fingers of one hand and use the thumb to press the wire against the mandrel. Then, using your thumb as a support and guide, rotate the handle with your other hand to wind the wire on to the mandrel. When you have become familiar with the action, you will find that you can use your index finger to spin the handle smoothly and continuously.

It is important that the wire is drawn off the reel without kinking, so do not allow the wire to loop off its reel. If the wire is blister-packed, make a hole in the packaging and pull the wire out though this hole. Alternatively, you could make a reel holder by fixing a length of dowel into a wooden base.

When the 'spring' of wire is long enough, use side cutters to snip each end then gently ease the spring off the mandrel. If the spring does not come off easily, hold it in one hand then rotate the mandrel in the reverse direction to 'unscrew' the mandrel from the spring.

Flattening wire springs

Having removed the wire spring from the mandrel, gently pull it apart, maintaining even spaces between each loop. Lay the opened spring on a hard surface and flatten one end with your finger. Carefully run the lino roller over the spring to flatten all the loops. The flattened spring will curve upwards at each end and it can be left like this if it is to be used for a necklet. If the spring is to be used on a card, however, turn it over and use the lino roller again to flatten out this curve.

At this stage you can change the length of the flattened spring by manually pulling the loops apart or pushing them together.

making an eye on the end of a wire

diagram 1   diagram 2

diagram 3   a   b   c

Making an eye on the end of wire

Grip the end of the wire with needle-nosed pliers (diagram 1) and turn the pliers in the direction shown to form an open eye (diagram 2). Remove the pliers, hold the wire vertically, then re-insert the pliers as shown in diagram 3a. Gently turn the pliers in the direction shown until the open eye is central to the wire (diagram 3b). Finally, squeeze the sides of the open eye to close it (diagram 3c).

Using a wire jig

Again, there are several types of wire jigs but, essentially, each jig consists of a grid of holes into which different diameter pegs can be placed. Normally, 19–23SWG wire can be used with wire jigs. Set up the jig by placing the appropriate size of pegs into the holes to match the project pattern (or your own design). Insert the end of the wire in a spare hole close to the peg at the start point of the design. Then, holding the reel of wire in one hand and releasing short lengths at a time, work the wire round the pegs. You will find it easier to turn the jig rather than the wire as you work through the design; this method also helps avoid unsightly kinks in thicker gauge wire. When the winding is complete, cut the wire and lift the winding off the jig. Twist the ends into place (or make eyelets) and snip off any excess wire.

Flattening wire designs made on a jig

When a wire design has been removed from the jig it must be pulled into its final shape and flattened. Place the wire design on to a hard surface, then use a nylon-headed hammer to flatten it. Turn it over and hammer it again. Repeat the turning and hammering until the design is perfectly flat. You can also use nylon-jaw, flat-nosed pliers to flatten small designs.

Making wire spirals

Some wire jigs have a special peg for making spirals, but you can easily create your own by making a hole in a 17mm diameter plastic peg with a large needle. Place the peg (with the small locating pin uppermost) on a firm surface. Holding the needle with a pair of insulated tweezers, heat its sharp end in a flame then push the needle into the plastic close to the locating pin as shown in the diagram below. Some pegs do have small holes created during the moulding process, but usually these are not close enough to the locating pin.

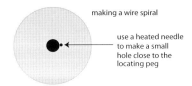

making a wire spiral

use a heated needle to make a small hole close to the locating peg

To make the spiral, push the end of the wire into the small hole, bend the wire flat against the bottom of the peg, then insert the peg into the centre hole of the jig. Now, holding the peg down with your finger, rotate the peg to wrap the wire round on itself. Continue rotating until the spiral is large enough. You can, of course, make a spiral on each end of a length of wire.

Making wire twists

You can twist two lengths of wire by hand, but it is better to use a hand drill and a cup hook. Screw the cup hook into a firm support at waist height. Cut a length of wire and secure both ends into the chuck of the drill. Place the loop of wire over the cup hook, pull the wire taut, then slowly rotate the drill to start twisting the wire. Keeping the wire under tension, continue rotating the drill until the twist is even over the whole length.

To make a double twist, cut two lengths of wire, place all four ends in the drill and rotate the drill at a slower speed to control the twist.

Attaching wire shapes on to cards

The best way to fix wire shapes on to card is to sew them on with fine gold, silver or coloured thread. Start by holding the work on the card, then use a needle tool to pierce holes on each side of the wire at strategic points. Use sticky tape to secure one end of a length of thread on the back of the card, then sew through the pierced holes to attach the wire to the card. Add any beads or sequins as required. Finish by securing the last stitch on the back of the card with sticky tape.

My designs are often layered, so the wire shape is sewn on to a loose piece of card which is then attached to the base card (or a lower layer) with double-sided sticky tape. If you sew the wire shape directly on to the base card, cut another piece of the same card slightly smaller (say 5mm all round) than the base card, and attach this with double-sided sticky tape on the inside of the base card to hide the stitches.

Adding texture to metal

There are various methods for creating a textured surface on metal.

You can make a simple texturing mallet by applying dots of glue from a hot-glue gun to the face of a wooden or rubber mallet. When the glue has cooled and hardened, place the sheet of metal on an embossing mat and hammer the texture on to the front or back of the metal.

Wooden meat tenderizers can also be used to create some interesting textures.

You can use a paper embossing tool and a stippling technique to create a series of small random dots.

Different sizes of modellers' miniature drill bits fitted in a clutch pencil can be used to make squiggles on the surface. Holding the pencil upright, apply light pressure on the metal and rotate the drill bit so that the teeth scratch the surface. Practise this technique on a spare piece of metal first, because if you press too hard you drill through the metal.

Embossing on metal

You can use embossing techniques to create raised or impressed images on metal.

For freehand designs, lay the sheet of metal on an embossing mat and use the tools specified in the project instructions to emboss the design on either the back or the front of the metal.

When using embossing stencils, first secure the stencil to the right side of the metal with small pieces of low-tack sticky tape. Place the metal on an embossing mat, then use an embossing tool to impress all the outlines of the design. Leaving the stencil in position, turn the metal over and check that all the outlines are raised slightly on the back. Now, working on the embossing mat, use a paper stump to emboss the spaces between the outlines.

Straight lines of embossed or impressed dots can be created using a plastic embossing wheel and ruler.

Using Friendly Plastic

This is a plastic material which, when heated, can be impressed with rubber-stamped images, wire, sequins or pieces of metal.

Use sharp heavy-duty scissors to cut the plastic to size, place the plastic (shiny side up) on an embossing craft sheet (or baking sheet), then place this on a thick wad of paper or an old telephone directory to protect the work surface. Apply a heat gun until the shiny surface starts to become crackled, then impress a rubber stamp into the heated surface. Leave the stamp in place until the plastic cools, then peel the plastic off the stamp. If you want to impress a coloured image, ink up the stamp (and leave it on the ink pad) before you start heating the plastic.

Wire, sequins and pieces of metal can be embedded in a similar manner, but you will have to reheat the plastic for each piece that you inset. Take care not to overheat the plastic as it will melt out of shape.

GREETINGS CARDS

GOLD BOX CARD (opposite, below right)

This card is made from a cardboard pencil box and makes an unusual gift. For a unique Silver or Golden Wedding Anniversary present, combine a small wedding photograph with a recent picture of the couple and attach both to the inside of the box with metal numerals (25 or 50). Alternatively, the box can take the form of a miniature shrine. Small 'found' items can be attached to the inside of the box, making a three-dimensional collage.

You will need
- cardboard pencil box
- gold coloured metal sheet
- strip of Friendly Plastic (turquoise/blue)
- gold and dark blue wire wound on different mandrels of a wire winder
- rubber stamp and permanent dye ink pad
- flat-backed, push mould polymer-clay head
- Brush 'n' Leaf (gold leaf)
- double-sided sticky tape
- high-tack glue
- Foil-it, 7cm wide self-adhesive gold tape
- **Optional:** decorative gold craft stickers for corners and narrow borders

Covering the box
As all boxes differ in shape and size, follow the diagrams and instructions below to make a paper pattern for your box.

Making paper patterns
Measure the box inside and out. Begin by drawing the pattern for the inside lining and front edge of the box. Measure from the hinge down the inside back wall, across the base, up the inside front wall and down the outside front wall to the base, then measure the length of the box and add 1cm (0.5cm allowance for folds at each side).

Next, draw the side lining pattern. Measure the side of the box, then measure from the base up the inside side wall and down the outside side wall.

Now draw the outside lining pattern. With the lid closed, measure from the front top edge of the box across the lid, over the hinge, down the back and across the base, and add 1cm (0.5cm allowance for folds at each end). Measure the length of the box and add 1cm (0.5cm allowance for folds at each side).

Finally, draw the pattern for the inside of the box lid (excluding the hinge), which should be 4mm shorter than the width and length of the lid.

Use the paper patterns to cut out the various metal pieces, remembering that you will need two side panels. Use a fine ball tool to score the fold lines. Cut small triangles of metal from the allowances at each fold point. If you wish, emboss simple patterns on to the metal, then fold the metal and dry fit the pieces to the box.

Gold Box Card
Making paper patterns (not to scale)

measuring box lining side view

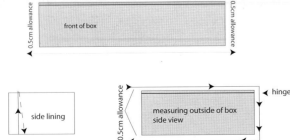

0.5cm allowance

front of box

0.5cm allowance

side lining

0.5cm allowance

measuring outside of box side view

hinge

Applying the outer lining

Spread high-tack glue over the exterior of the lid, back and base of the box, then, leaving the 0.5cm allowance at the front edge of the lid, smooth the metal over the lid, back and base. Ensure that the metal is firmly adhered. Apply more glue to the flaps, then smooth them over the top and side edges of the lid and round on to the sides and front of the box. Use a lino roller to create sharp edges on all corners.

Applying the front and inner lining

Spread high-tack glue over the inside back, the inside base and the inside and outside of the front of the box. Starting at the bottom of the front of the box, smooth the metal on to the front, over the top edge, down the inside front, across the base and up the inside back of the box. If necessary, add more glue to stick the flaps down on the insides of the box and round on to the outside sides of the box. Again use the lino roller to create sharp edges.

Applying the side and lid linings

Ensure that all flaps are firmly secure, attach the metal to the two sides and the underside of the lid, then use the lino roller to ensure they are firmly attached.

Finishing off

Apply self-adhesive gold strip over the inside hinge area to cover exposed edges of the linings. If you are using craft stickers, adhere them firmly to the box corners and edges after the box is covered.

Tip: The project box has a lip around the outer edges; a slightly more generous allowance and neat snipping at the corners will cover these.

Decorating the box

Paint the polymer-clay head with Brush 'n' Leaf. Heat and texture the Friendly Plastic with a rubber stamp (see page 7). Re-heat the central area of the plastic, then push the gold and blue wire and head firmly into place. When the plastic is completely cool, use double-sided sticky tape to attach it on the front of the box.

GOLD SPIRALS CARD (see page 9, left)

You will need
- 23 and 27SWG gold wire
- wire jig with spiral peg (see page 6)
- wire winder with 3mm mandrel
- A4 and A5 sheet of dark blue card
- double-sided sticky tape
- needle and gold thread
- needle tool and perforating mat

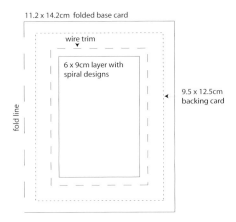

Gold Spirals Card
Enlarge pattern by 200%

Instructions

Use 23SWG gold wire and the wire jig to make five single-ended spirals (see page 6). Wind a full mandrel of 27SWG gold wire on the winder and flatten (see page 5). Fold the A4 card in half and trim to 11.2 x 14.2cm. Cut a 9.5 x 12.5cm backing card and a 6 x 9cm centre layer from the A5 card. Using the small piece of card as a guide, pierce an outline of holes in the base card with a needle tool, then stitch on the flattened spiral. Arrange and attach the individual spirals on the front. Insert the layer into the frame and attach with double-sided sticky tape. Finally, position the backing card on the inside of the folded card to conceal the stitches.

COPPER WIRE AND METAL CARD
(see page 9, top)

You will need
- A4 and A5 sheet of dark green card
- 12.6cm square of copper coloured metal
- texturing mallet
- 19 and 23SWG copper wire and a wire jig
- three small pearls
- needle and fine thread
- needle tool and perforating mat
- double-sided sticky tape

Instructions
Referring to the diagram below, fold and trim the A4 sheet of card to form a 14.6cm folded square. Texture the piece of copper (see page 7), and secure it on the front of the card with double-sided sticky tape. Set up the wire jig as shown in the diagram opposite, then use 19SWG copper wire to wind the shape. Remove the wire shape from the jig, curve the ends round neatly and cut off excess. Gently stretch the design until it is 8cm in length. Flatten the shape (see page 6).

Use 23SWG copper wire to make one double-ended and one single-ended spiral. Cut a 9.6cm square from the A5 piece of card and arrange the wire windings on it. Pierce holes and sew the shapes into place. Add a small pearl in the centre of each spiral. Use double-sided sticky tape to secure the finished layer to the copper.

Copper Wire and Metal Card

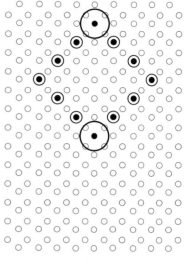

peg placement

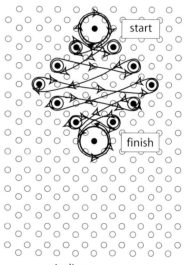

winding sequence

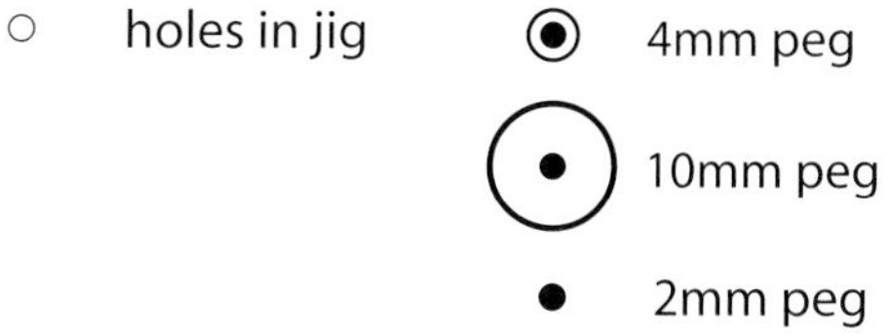

Copper Wire and Metal Card
Enlarge pattern by 200%

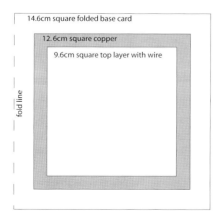

○   holes in jig   ◉   4mm peg

⦿   10mm peg

●   2mm peg

Wire Mesh and Silver Metal Punched Card
Enlarge pattern by 200%

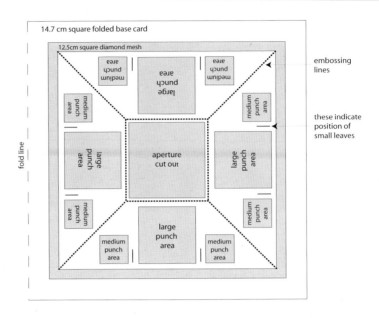

14.7 cm square folded base card

12.5cm square diamond mesh

medium punch area

medium punch area

large punch area

medium punch area

medium punch area

large punch area

aperture cut out

large punch area

medium punch area

medium punch area

large punch area

medium punch area

medium punch area

fold line

embossing lines

these indicate position of small leaves

WIRE MESH AND SILVER METAL PUNCHED CARD (see front cover)

You will need
- silver coloured metal
- 12.5cm square of 6mm diamond mesh
- A4 and A5 sheet of dark blue card
- maple leaf punches – large, medium and small
- embossing wheel, fine embossing tool and embossing mat
- Fiskars deckle-edged paper scissors
- heavy-duty craft knife and cutting board
- high-tack glue and a cocktail stick
- double-sided sticky tape
- permanent marker
- **Optional:** power punch

Instructions

Cut a 12,5cm square of silver metal. Referring to the diagram above, use the embossing wheel to emboss the lines on the metal (see page 7). Use a heavy-duty knife to cut out the centre aperture. Punch four large and eight medium-size leaves around the edge of the metal. Save the punched out leaves. Punch another large leaf and eight small ones from a spare piece of silver metal. Although you can punch the leaves by hand, a power punch will make this task much easier. Use a fine embossing tool to create veins on all of the punched out leaves.

Fold and trim the A4 sheet of card to form a 14.7cm folded square. Working 1cm in from the edges, sew the diamond mesh to the base card. Turn the punched metal square over, then use a permanent marker to draw a line 0.5cm in from each edge. Trim along these lines with deckle-edged scissors. Use the high-tack glue to secure the punched metal square on the wire mesh and to attach the small punched leaves as shown in the diagram.

Cut a 12.5cm square from the A5 sheet of card, then use strips of double-sided sticky tape to attach this on the inside the card to conceal the stitches.

GREETINGS CARDS WITH CRAFT STICKERS

Decorative craft stickers combine with metal and fine wire mesh to make
unusual and classy-looking cards. There is a huge choice of designs, so you
should have no trouble in finding exactly the right one for that special occasion.

SILVER MOORISH DESIGN CARD
(see front cover, bottom right)

As soon as I saw the craft sticker used in this project I new exactly how I wanted to use one of the designs on a card. I used most of the design, removing it piece by piece from the backing paper and reassembling the design on to a sheet of silver metal. I then embellished the exposed areas of metal with embossing.

You will need
- craft sticker (Starform sheet No. 924, silver)
- tweezers
- silver coloured metal
- embossing tools and foam mat
- A4 and A5 sheet of dark blue card
- double-sided and low-tack sticky tape
- piece of white paper
- lino roller

Instructions
Referring to the diagram below, cut an aperture mask from the white paper. The size of the aperture is the same as one of the complete designs on the craft sticker sheet. Use low-tack tape to attach this mask to the silver metal.

Using the aperture mask as a guide, transfer the craft sticker design on to the silver metal. Use tweezers to carefully remove each segment of the design, leaving behind the waste parts. Start with the corner and side pieces, then apply the other segments of the design, ensuring that the spaces between each are maintained. For this card, I omitted three of the central clover leaf shapes.

Cut the metal to its finished size (10.5 x 12cm) by trimming round the outline of the paper mask. Place the metal face on a hard, smooth surface, then run the lino roller over the stickers several times to ensure they are firmly attached.

Working on the foam mat, use a fine ball tool and a paper stump to stipple and emboss the exposed parts of the silver metal. I used an ultra-fine ball tool to create the lines emanating from the centre star of three of the shapes.

Silver Moorish Design Card
Enlarge pattern by 200%

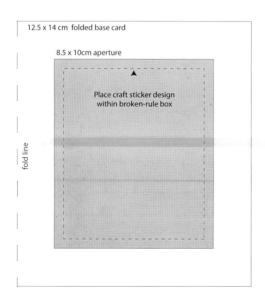

12.5 x 14 cm folded base card

8.5 x 10cm aperture

Place craft sticker design
within broken-rule box

fold line

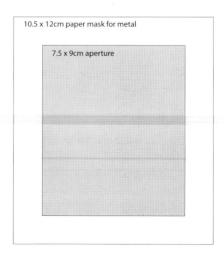

10.5 x 12cm paper mask for metal

7.5 x 9cm aperture

Fold and trim the A4 sheet of card to 12.5 x 14cm, then cut an 8.5 x 10cm aperture in the front of the card (see diagram opposite). Place double-sided sticky tape close to the edges around the back of the aperture. Remove the protective paper and, with the right side of the card facing you, centre the aperture over the silver design and stick the card to the silver sheet. Trim the A5 sheet of card to 11.5 x 13cm and use double-sided sticky tape to attach this on the inside front to give a neat finish.

GOLD METAL MASK
(see page 13, bottom left)

You will need
- craft sticker (Starform sheet No. 947, gold)
- tweezers
- gold coloured metal
- embossing tools and foam mat
- A4 and A5 sheet of crimson card
- gold paper
- double-sided sticky tape
- lino roller
- heavy-duty craft knife and cutting mat
- heavy-duty scissors

Instructions
Use tweezers to carefully remove the craft sticker (see page 13, bottom left) from the backing sheet, leaving the solid eye shapes behind, and position it on the gold metal. Place the metal face up on a hard, smooth surface and run the lino roller over it to secure the sticker. Taking care that the knife does not slip on the metal, use the craft knife and cutting mat to make horizontal and vertical cuts across the centre of each eye shape. Use heavy-duty scissors to cut away the metal round each eye. Referring to the photograph, decorate the exposed parts of the gold metal. Place the metal on the foam mat, then use a fine ball tool to draw a line around the mask approximately 0.7cm from the outer edge. Stipple the head, using a large ball tool for large areas and a fine ball tool for smaller areas. Use the fine ball tool to trace the main

contours of the design, including the eyelashes. Turn the metal over and use a paper stump to raise the petal and teardrop shapes on the forehead, the end of the nose, the lips, the shapes on either side of the lips and the two curlicue shapes on the chin. Turn the metal over and use an embossing wheel to define the sides of the face. Use a drill bit to emboss star shapes in the six circles in the lower half of the face. Complete the decoration by using a fine ball tool to stipple a border round the mask. Use heavy-duty scissors to cut out the mask.

Fold and trim the A4 card to 13.7 x 16.7cm. Cut a 9.7 x 12.7cm rectangle from the gold paper and an 8.7 x 11.7cm rectangle from the A5 piece of card. Use double-sided sticky tape to layer the gold paper and the card rectangles on the front of the folded card. Finally, use double-sided sticky tape to attach the gold mask.

SILVER MASK (see page 13, top right)

You will need
- craft sticker (Starform sheet No. 947, silver)
- tweezers
- silver coloured metal
- embossing tools and foam mat
- texturing mallet
- A4 and A5 sheet of dark blue card
- double-sided sticky tape
- lino roller
- heavy-duty craft knife and cutting mat
- heavy-duty scissors
- Paint Jewels – blue tanzanite; sapphire; citrine yellow and crystal pink

Instructions
Carefully remove the craft sticker from its backing sheet, leaving behind the eye shapes, and position on the silver metal. Place the metal (sticker side up) on to a hard, smooth surface, then run the lino roller over it to secure the sticker. Referring to the previous project, use the heavy-duty craft knife and cutting mat, and the heavy-duty scissors to cut the eye shapes. Place the metal, face up, on the foam mat and use a fine ball tool to trace the

main contours of the face. Turn the metal over and use a paper stump to raise the turban, the flowers, the lips, the end of nose and the flower decoration. Turn your work over again (sticker side up) and, referring to the photograph on page 13, use a fine ball tool to make dotted lines along the top or bottom line of the folds of the turban and to stipple where the folds overlap. These marks help create shadows and add depth to the turban. Stipple the centre of the flowers and the shapes around the flower decoration. Use a drill bit to create star shapes in the centres of the decoration at the left-hand side of the face.

When all the embossing is complete, squeeze some blue paint in the recesses of the turban and flower decoration, then use a brush to spread the paint evenly. Use the remaining colours to decorate other parts of the design. When the paints are completely dry, use heavy-duty scissors to cut round the outside edge of the mask.

Fold and trim the A4 sheet of card to 14.3 x 17cm. Cut a 9.1 x 12cm rectangle from the A5 sheet of card, and an 11.1 x 14cm rectangle from the silver metal. Lay the metal on the foam mat and use the texturing mallet to decorate a 1cm border on each edge. Use double-sided sticky tape to layer the textured silver metal and the blue rectangles on the front of the folded card, then attach the silver mask.

GOLD MESH MASK
(see page 13, top left)

The mask sticker used for this card is part of a larger design that includes a moon and a star. It is separated by cutting through the bridges which link it to the other parts.

You will need
- craft stickers (Starform sheets Nos. 946 and 947, gold)
- tweezers
- gold coloured wire mesh
- gold coloured metal
- gold paper
- embossing tools and foam mat
- A4 and A5 sheet of crimson card
- texturing mallet
- Fiskars paper edgers – Victorian design
- double-sided sticky tape
- lino roller
- sharp, pointed scalpel
- permanent marker

Instructions
Cut a 10 x 13cm piece of gold wire mesh, place it on to a smooth, hard surface and roll it on both sides with the lino roller until it is straight and flat. Referring to the photograph on page 13, use the scalpel to cut through the bridges that connect the mask to the other parts of the design. Carefully remove the mask (making sure that all the bridges are cleanly severed), then attach it to the wire mesh, leaving space for the other sticker to be added. Carefully remove the small mask (I used the one with heart shapes from sheet 947, but you could use one of those on sheet 946) and attach this to the wire mesh. Work the lino roller over the front and back of the wire mesh several times to ensure the stickers are firmly attached.

Cut out the eye shapes from the large mask and then cut around the outer edges of both masks following the outline of the stickers.

Fold and trim the A4 card to 14.8 x 17.4cm. Cut a 9.8 x 12.3cm rectangle from the gold paper and an 8.8 x 11.3cm rectangle from the A5 piece of card. Cut an 8.8 x 11.3cm and a 3 x 3.8cm rectangle from the gold metal.

Turn the large piece of gold metal over and use a permanent marker to draw a line 0.5cm in from each edge. Use the paper edgers to cut along these lines. Lay both pieces of metal on the foam pad and use the texture mallet to decorate them.

Use double-sided tape to layer the gold paper, the red card, the large piece of textured gold metal and the large mask centrally on the folded card. Referring to the photograph on page 13, stick the small piece of gold metal on the bottom, right-hand corner of the central layers then attach the small mask. Use the lino roller to ensure that all layers are firmly joined together.

TRIANGLE CARD
(see page 13, bottom right)

You will need
- craft sticker (Starform sheet No. 2209, gold)
- tweezers
- gold coloured metal
- embossing tools and foam mat
- A4 and A5 sheet of crimson card
- gold paper
- double-sided sticky tape
- lino roller

Instructions
Referring to the diagram below cut a triangle from the gold metal, then attach one of the small triangular sticker designs in the centre. Place the metal (sticker side up) on to a hard, smooth surface and run the lino roller over it several times. Place the metal on the foam mat (sticker side up) and use a fine ball tool to trace round the inside contours of the five diamond shapes that surround the central star, and round the outer shapes of the triangle. Turn the metal over and use a paper stump to raise these areas. Turn the metal (sticker side up), then use a fine ball tool to decorate the inner shapes with delicate lines, and to stipple the areas of the star. Use a medium ball tool to stipple the area around the outside of the sticker.

Referring to the diagram on page 18, cut out the triangular card with an aperture, and cut the gold paper as a border trim. Use double-sided sticky tape to attach the gold trim to the front of the card (see photograph on page 13). Use double-sided sticky tape, attached along the back edges of the aperture, to fix the metal design in place. Cut a backing piece from the A5 piece of card, then attach this over the back of the metal to complete the card.

Triangle Card
Enlarge pattern by 200%

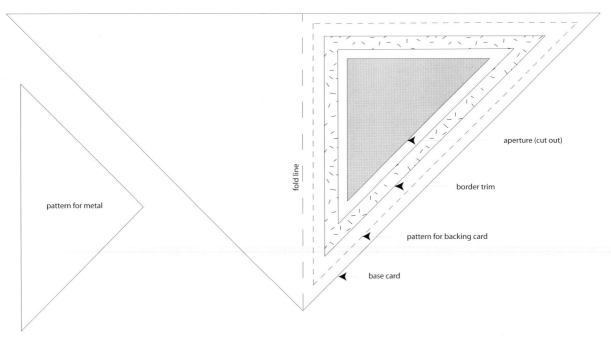

pattern for metal

fold line

aperture (cut out)

border trim

pattern for backing card

base card

WIRE EMBROIDERY ON METAL AND MESH

I am indebted to Erica Fortgens, the leading designer and pioneer of paper
embroidery, for allowing me to convert some of her early patterns.
Paper embroidery has become very popular in recent years, so, especially for fans
of paper embroidery, here is my version of paper embroidery on metal and mesh.

RED WIRE ON SILVER METAL LEAF CARD (see page 17, bottom)

You will need
- 30SWG red wire
- silver coloured metal
- A4 sheet of crimson card
- piece of mount board (or 2mm thick card)
- embossing tools, needle tool and foam pad
- single and double-sided sticky tape
- tracing paper (90gsm)

Instructions
Enlarge the embroidery pattern below by 200%,
photocopy or trace it on to tracing paper, then
attach this on the silver metal with low-tack sticky
tape. Place the metal on the foam mat and use the
needle tool to pierce all the holes. Cut a length of
red wire and push this through from the back of
the work at point A1 on the pattern. Use sticky
tape to secure the end of the wire to the metal.
Follow the pattern and work one corner of the
design at a time. Snip off excess lengths of wire
and tidy up the ends by sticking them to the back
of the metal. None of the wire ends must extend
across areas to be embossed.

Referring to the embossing guide, use a plastic
embossing wheel and a ruler to emboss the border
round the embroidery (see diagram). Use a fine
ball tool to emboss and stipple the leaf shapes,
then trim the metal to size.

Cut an 8.4cm square of mount board, position
this on the back of the decorated metal, then
carefully smooth the edges of the metal up and
over the mount board to make a snug fit.

Fold and trim the A4 sheet of card to an 11.6cm
square, then use double-sided sticky tape to mount
the embroidered metal plaque on the front.

COPPER METAL AND GREEN WIRE CARD (see page 17, top)

You will need
- 30SWG green wire   28ga
- copper coloured metal
- A4 sheet of dark green card
- embossing tools and foam pad
- texturing mallet
- needle tool
- single and double-sided sticky tape
- tracing paper (90gsm)
- skeleton leaf stamp and green dye ink pad

Red wire on Silver Metal Leaf Card. Enlarge pattern by 200%

embroidery pattern

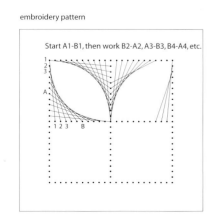

Start A1-B1, then work B2-A2, A3-B3, B4-A4, etc.

embossing guide

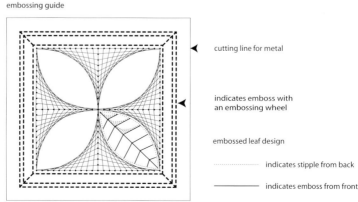

◀ cutting line for metal

◀ indicates emboss with an embossing wheel

embossed leaf design

.... indicates stipple from back

————— indicates emboss from front

Copper Metal and Green Wire Card
Enlarge pattern by 200%

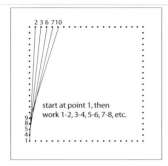

embroidery pattern

embossing guide

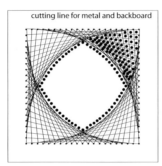

cutting line for metal and backboard

Instructions

Enlarge the embroidery pattern above on to tracing paper, then secure it to the copper metal. Place the metal on the foam mat and use the needle tool to pierce all the holes. Cut a length of green wire and push this through the back at point 1. Tape the end of the wire to the metal, then referring to the pattern, work one corner of the design at a time. Snip off excess lengths of wire and tidy up the ends by sticking them to the back of the metal. None of the wire ends must extend across areas to be embossed.

Trim the metal to an 8.2cm square, lay it on the foam pad and use the mallet to add texture to the area between the embroidery and the edge of the metal. Referring to the photograph on page 17, use a large embossing tool to emboss evenly-spaced dots round the inner edges of the embroidery and others in the mesh of the embroidery. Turn the metal over and use an embossing tool to raise the centre area.

Fold and trim the A4 card to an 11.2cm square, then cut an 8.2cm square for a backing card. Stamp a random skeleton leaf stamp pattern on the front face of the folded card. Use double-sided sticky tape to attach the metal to the backing card and the backing card to the folded card.

GREEN METAL AND GOLD WIRE EMBROIDERY CARD
(see page 17, middle)

You will need
- 33SWG gold wire
- green coloured metal
- A4 and A5 sheets of ivory card with gold back (Lacé)
- embossing tools and foam mat
- needle tool
- single and double-sided sticky tape
- tracing paper (90gsm)

Instructions

Enlarge the embroidery pattern on page 22 by 200%, photocopy or trace it on to a piece of tracing paper, then use low-tack tape to secure the pattern on the green metal. Place the metal on the foam mat, then use the needle tool to pierce all the holes (for clarity, the pattern only shows odd-numbered holes, but you must also pierce holes for the even numbers). Cut a length of gold wire and push this through from the back at point 1 on the pattern. Attach the end of the wire to the metal with a piece of sticky tape. Referring to the pattern, work right round the design, bringing the wire up through the odd numbers and down through the even numbers. Snip off excess lengths of wire and tidy up the ends by sticking them to the back of the metal. None of the wire ends must extend across areas to be embossed. Trim the metal to a 9.9cm square

Place the metal on the foam mat, then, referring to the photograph on page 17, use a plastic embossing wheel and a ruler to emboss the diamond grid design. Use a large drill bit to emboss the star shapes in the centre of the design. Use a fine ball tool to emboss straight lines between the stars.

Fold and trim the A4 card (so that the gold face is on the inside) to a 14.8cm square. Cut an 11.9cm square from the A5 card, then, using the gold side as the front, cut an 8.9cm aperture in this piece of card. Use double-sided sticky tape to attach the embroidery behind the aperture, then the mounted embroidery on to the folded card.

Green Metal and Gold Wire embroidery Card
Enlarge pattern by 200%

embroidery and embossing pattern

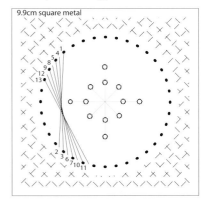

9.9cm square metal

making the card

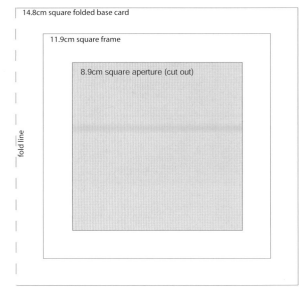

14.8cm square folded base card

11.9cm square frame

8.9cm square aperture (cut out)

fold line

GOLD MESH AND METAL
CIRCULAR BOX (see page 21, top)

Although the pattern for this project is sized for a 16cm diameter x 5cm deep box, it can be enlarged or reduced to fit other sizes.

You will need
- 16cm diameter x 5cm deep circular chipwood or papier mâché box
- Brush 'n' Leaf gold leaf
- brush
- sheet of gold wire mesh
- sheet of gold metal
- 30SWG red wire
- five green flower beads and five gold coloured glass rocaille beads
- needle and gold thread
- A3 sheet of thin gold hologram card
- embossing tools and foam pad
- needle tool
- texturing mallet
- cocktail stick
- normal and low-tack sticky tape
- double-sided sticky sheets and tape
- tracing paper (90gsm)
- lino roller

Tip: When covering boxes bear in mind that any decoration on the sides of the box must allow space for the box lid to close (see page 21).

Instructions
Paint the box inside and out with gold leaf. Enlarge the embroidery pattern by 200%, then photocopy or trace it on to a piece of tracing paper. Cut 14cm circles from the wire mesh, the hologram card and the high-tack, double-sided sticky sheet.

Use low tack tape to attach the hologram card on the back of the wire mesh (with the hologram effect showing through the mesh) and the traced pattern on the front. Place the mesh on the foam mat, then, referring to the pattern on page 23, use the needle tool to pierce the holes (including those for the bead decoration) through the mesh and card.

Cut a length of red wire and push this through from the back at point A1 on the pattern. Attach the end of the wire to the back of the card with a piece of sticky tape. Referring to the pattern, work one shape at a time. Snip off excess lengths of wire and tidy up the ends by sticking them to the back of the card.

Bring the gold thread up through the card and mesh (securing the end with sticky tape), pass it through a green flower bead and a rocaille bead, back through the flower bead and down through the mesh and card. Repeat with the other four sets of beads.

Gold Mesh and Metal Circular Box
Enlarge pattern by 200%

embroidery pattern

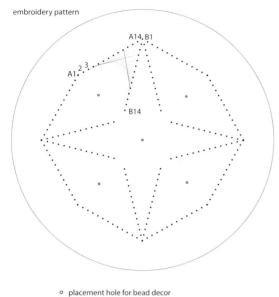

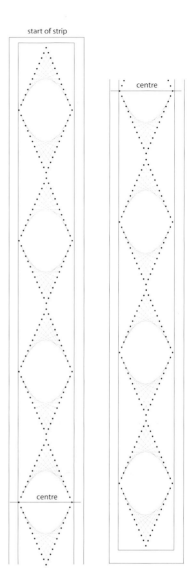

start of strip

centre

centre

stitching ends of lid edge mesh to box

outside lid

inside lid

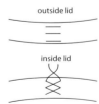

○   placement hole for bead decor

——   ——   cutting line for embroidered piece

— — — — —   score line for lid edge

pattern for metal on box lid

cut along solid lines
up to the dashed line

cut out these areas
around the whole
of the edge.

Attach the circle of double-sided sticky sheet to the card on the back of the embroidery, then attach the embroidery to the box lid.

Cut an 17.8cm diameter circle from the gold metal, then cut a 7.5cm diameter aperture in the middle. Enlarge the metal pattern for the lid (above) by 200%, then use low-tack tape to secure this to the metal. Use an embossing tool to draw the two dashed-line circles in the centre, then carefully cut out the tongues of metal. Draw in the outer dashed-line circle, then use the mallet to texture the area between the outer two circles. Use a 2cm length of cocktail stick to roll the large tongues of metal back to the drawn line. Bend the small tongues back under the metal to leave a neat safe edge. Cut out the triangles round the outer edge of the metal, then use double-sided tape to attach the metal to the lid. Stick a strip of double-sided tape around the side of the lid, then smooth the triangles down.

Cut a 2.6 x 51.5cm piece of wire mesh (or measure around the side of your box lid and add 1cm). Neaten the edges by turning over 0.5cm along each long side and 0.3cm on one short end. Use the lino roller to ensure that the edges are really sharp. Place a strip of double-sided tape around the side of the box lid, trimming it level with the top and bottom edges. Starting with the neat end, wrap the wire mesh around the side of the lid, stretching it to fit as you press down. As you work round to the start point, mark where one neat edge meets the other and tuck excess mesh under itself. Referring to the diagram on page 23, use a thicker gold thread (or several thin strands) to sew the ends of the mesh together through the lid itself. Knot the ends of thread together on the inside, then snip off excess thread.

Cut a 4 x 50.5cm piece of wire mesh and a 3 x 49cm piece of hologram card. Lay the card (plain side up) on the mesh and turn over 0.5cm of mesh on both of the long sides. Use the lino roller to sharpen the edges. Turn 0.3cm of one end of the mesh over the card as well. Mark the centre of the card with a pencil, then turn the whole thing over, mesh side up. Enlarge the side strip embroidery pattern on page 23 and make a tracing paper pattern. Match up the centres of the embroidery pattern and the mesh, then pierce the design through both layers. Use red wire to embroider the design along the strip. Place 2.8cm wide strips of double-sided sticky sheet on the outside of the box, close to the bottom edge. Starting with the neat end, wrap the embroidered strip round the box (as for the lid). Stitch the two ends together as before but, this time, use four stitches on the outside and tuck the thread ends out of sight.

BLUE AND SILVER BOX
(see page 21, bottom)

You will need
- wooden cigar box (interior dimensions 170 x 120 x 47mm)
- sapphire coloured metal
- silver coloured metal
- 30SWG silver wire
- paper serviette and collage adhesive
- embossing tools and foam mat
- needle tool
- texturing mallet
- self-adhesive silver metal tape
- low-tack sticky tape
- double-sided sticky sheet and tape
- tracing paper (90gsm)
- lino roller

Instructions
Collage the inside of the box using a pretty paper serviette. Enlarge the box patterns on page 26 by 200%, then photocopy or trace on to tracing paper. Cut a 17.7 x 12.8cm piece of sapphire metal, use low-tack tape to attach the embroidery pattern to the metal, then use the needle tool to pierce the holes for the embroidery design. While the pattern is still attached, use a ruler and plastic embossing wheel to emboss the diamond pattern on each side of the embroidery area. Remove the pattern, then, referring to the diagram on page 26 and the photograph on page 21, use silver wire to embroider the design. Work one half of the design at a time, starting with triangle A and ending with triangle H. Use a drill bit to emboss star shapes in the diamond pattern.

Cut a 17.7 x 12.8 piece of silver metal, then cut a 13.8 x 8.9cm aperture in the middle. Place the frame pattern on the metal and use a fine ball embossing tool to draw in the fold lines (see diagram on page 26). Snip diagonals from the corners of the aperture to the fold line, fold the flaps under and use the lino roller to create sharp edges. Use the mallet to add texture to the frame.

Use a piece of double-sided sticky sheet to attach the embroidered metal to the lid. Use sticky tape to attach the silver metal frame. Cover the edge of the lid with self-adhesive silver metal tape. Start and finish at the back of the lid, aligning the

Blue and Silver Box. Enlarge patterns by 200%

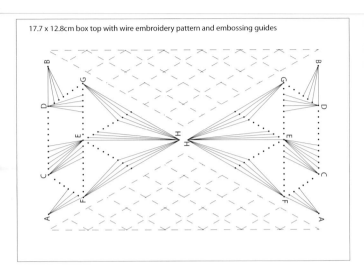

17.7 x 12.8cm box top with wire embroidery pattern and embossing guides

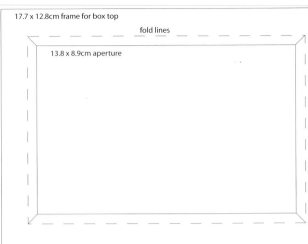

17.7 x 12.8cm frame for box top

fold lines

13.8 x 8.9cm aperture

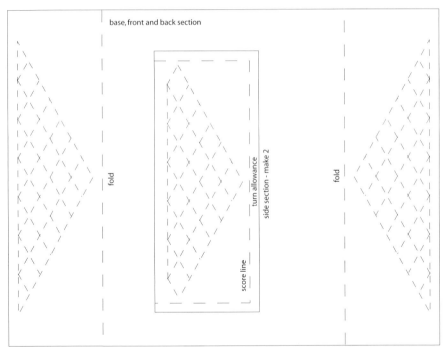

base, front and back section

fold

fold

score line

turn allowance

side section - make 2

tape with the bottom edge of the lid, and carefully stretch it right round the lid. Make small snips in the tape as it passes over the upper hinge. Smooth the tape over the edges of the frame, then firm down with a lino roller.

Cut the base, front and back section and two side sections (see diagram above) from the sapphire coloured metal. Use a ruler and plastic embossing wheel to emboss the diamond patterns and a fine ball tool to mark the fold lines. Use a

large drill bit to make star shapes in the diamond pattern. Use pieces of double-sided sticky sheet to secure the metal sides to the box. Mitre the bottom corners on each piece, then fold the flaps on to the front, back and bottom of the box. Firm down all edges with a lino roller. Use a piece of double-sided sticky sheet to fit the base, front and back section of the box. Starting at the top, front edge of this piece, smooth it down on the front, across the base and up the back. Use the lino roller to give nice sharp folds. Use a paper stump to smooth over the joins in the metal on each side and along the bottom edges of the box.

Use strips of self-adhesive silver metal tape to cover the remaining exposed top edges of the box. Align one edge of the tape with the outside edge of the top of the box, then smooth the tape down over the inside of the box. Work the other three sides in the same way. Now, starting at the middle of the back of the box, and allowing for the tape to fold across the top edges of the box, stick a long strip of tape round the top of the box. Snip the tape in the corners and on either side of the hinges, then smooth the tape down across the top (over the previous layer). Use the lino roller to firm down all edges.

FRAMES WITH METAL AND MESH

Metal and wire mesh make lovely and unusual photograph, picture or mirror frames.
All of the projects shown here are suitable for bought frames or to refurbish an old frame.
There are also tips on adapting the ideas for greetings cards.

COPPER MESH FRAME WITH METAL CORNERS (see page 25, bottom right)

The diagram on page 28 is the pattern for my photoframe, but it can be used as a guide to create a pattern for any size of frame. Remember that the flaps round the outside of the frame and the inside of the aperture must be sized to match the thickness of the frame.

You will need
- photoframe (mine measured 12 x 16cm)
- copper coloured wire mesh
- copper coloured metal
- brass embossing template
- Fiskars deckle-edged scissors
- double-sided sticky tape
- masking tape
- embossing tools and foam mat
- lino roller

Instructions
Carefully separate the frame from the glass and backing board. If your frame is glued, a sharp knife will slice through the join. Use the diagram on page 28 as a guide to draw a pattern to suit your frame, then use this to cut the copper mesh. Use strips of double-sided tape applied to the flaps round the outside of the frame and round the aperture, to secure the wire mesh to the frame. Use a lino roller to ensure that the mesh is held securely and that all edges are sharp.

Enlarge the corner pattern (see page 28) to fit your frame, then cut four of these shapes from the copper metal. Use deckle-edged scissors to cut the diagonal lines. Use a fine ball tool to make the fold lines. Use low-tack tape to position the brass template on the front face of the visible area of one of the corners (see photograph on page 25), then use a fine ball tool to draw round the outlines of the design. Leaving the template in place, turn the corner over and use a paper stump to raise the areas that you have embossed. Repeat this process with the other three corners.

Use a ruler, placed along the embossed fold lines, and your finger to fold the flaps. Check that the first corner fits the frame then repeat the process with the other three pieces. Use double-sided sticky tape to attach the corners to the mesh and the lino roller to sharpen the edges.

Use strips of sticky tape to secure the decorated frame to the backing board. If your frame is the type where the glass slides through the top, do not apply tape to this edge. Finally, slip the glass and your photograph into the frame.

Tip: You could use embossed metal corners to liven up a hand-made greetings card. Secure the metal corners to the top layer before attaching this to the base card.

Copper Mesh Frame with Metal Corners
Use these diagrams as guides to create patterns to
suit the size of your frame

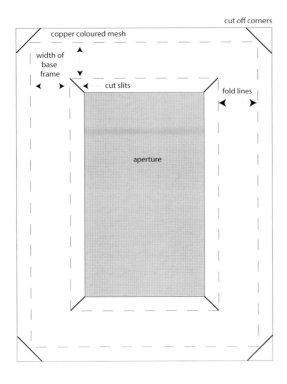

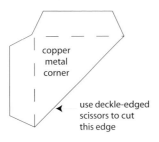

COPPER METAL FRAME WITH GOLD PUNCHED TRIM (see page 25, top)

Materials
- photoframe (mine measured 17 x 22cm)
- copper metal
- gold metal
- border punch
- fine point embossing tool
- double-sided sticky tape
- high-tack glue and a cocktail stick
- masking tape
- lino roller
- **Optional:** power punch

Instructions
Referring to the instructions for the previous project, take the frame apart and, using the diagram on page 30, prepare a pattern to suit your frame. Use this pattern to cut the copper metal to size. Use a fine ball tool to emboss the fold lines, then mitre the outer corners and the inner corners of the aperture. Use strips of double-sided tape, applied to the flaps round the outside of the frame and those round the aperture, to secure the copper metal to the frame. Use the lino roller to ensure that the metal is held securely and that all edges are sharp.

Cut four 2cm wide strips of gold metal; two of these 3cm longer than the width of the frame, and two 3cm longer than the height. Use the border punch to decorate each strip (see diagram on page 31 for the punch I used), then reduce the width of each strip to 1cm. Place the two short strips across the front of the frame, bend the ends down and round to the back, then remove them. Apply dabs of high-tack glue to the areas between the punched-out shapes, then position one strip at the top and one at the bottom of the frame, leaving a 0.7cm border between the strip and the outside edges of the frame. Press them into place. Attach the two long strips to each side of the frame in a similar manner. Use high-tack glue to secure the ends of all strips on the back of the frame. Leave the glue to dry, then, referring to the photograph on page 25, use a fine point embossing tool to stipple the areas of copper metal that are visible through the punched strips. Reassemble the frame as described in the previous project.

Copper Metal Frame with Gold Punched Trim.
Use this diagram as a guide to create a pattern to suit the size of your frame

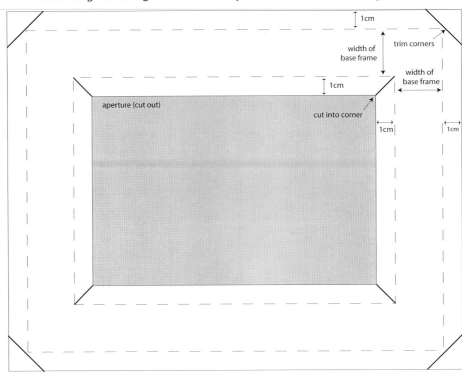

Idea for using a punched strip to decorate a greetings card (see page 25, left)

Extra materials
- A4 sheet of broken white textured card

Instructions
Referring to the diagram on page 31, fold and trim the A4 card to size. Cut a 3 x 20cm strip from the spare card. Cut a 2.3 x 22cm strip of copper metal, then use double-sided sticky tape to attach this to the front of the folded card, 1cm in from the outer edge. Cut a 2 x 22cm strip of gold metal, punch a design as described on page 28, and trim the width to 1cm. Use dabs of high-tack glue to stick the strip in the centre of the copper, then, when the glue is dry, stipple through the punched out shapes. Fold the ends of the copper and gold strip on to the inside front of the card and use the lino roller to make sharp folds. Use double-sided sticky tape to attach the strip of white card to the inside of the folded card to conceal the ends of the metal.

LARGE FRAME FOR A MIRROR OR A PICTURE (see page 29, top)

You will need
- MDF plain square frame 40 x 40cm (made to take a mirror 25 x 25cm)
- silver and gold coloured metal
- double-sided sticky sheets and tape
- cutting ruler, mat and strong craft knife
- texturing mallet
- embossing wheel and foam mat
- lino roller
- masking tape

Instructions
Referring to the diagrams on page 32 (top), cut four 1.5 x 18cm strips of gold and four of silver. Cut a 12 x 18cm piece of double-sided sticky sheet, remove the backing from one side, then stick the gold and silver strips alternately on to this. Cut eight 1.5cm strips, each with alternating blocks of gold and silver from this block (the spare pieces can be used for the next project). Use a

Copper Card with Punched Trim.
Enlarge pattern by 200%

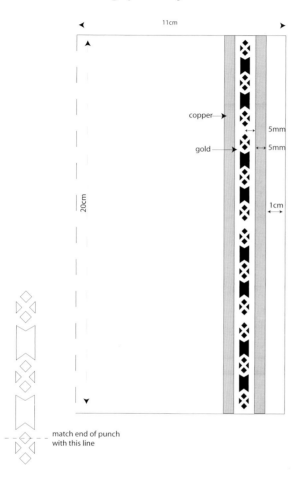

ruler and the embossing wheel to decorate the
edges of the strips. Repeat the above process to
make another three sets of strips, one set for each
corner decoration.

Working one corner at a time, build the strips
into a checkerboard pattern, taking the strips
round the edge of the frame on to the back.
Measure the spaces between the corners, then cut
four pieces of gold metal to fit these spaces; the
width of these pieces should allow for the sides of
each piece to be folded round on to the back of
the frame. Use the mallet to texture all four pieces,
then use pieces of double-sided sticky sheet to
stick the pieces between the checkerboard
corners. Fold the flaps round to the back of the
frame, then cover their edges with strips of
masking tape.

CHECKERBOARD BORDER CARD
(see page 29. bottom)

You will need
- left-over gold/silver strips from the previous project
- 7 x 10.5cm piece of diamond mesh
- approximately six silver star beads
- 27SWG gold wire
- gold thread and a needle
- A4 and A5 sheet of teal coloured card
- double-sided sticky tape

Instructions
Fold and trim the A4 card to 14.5 x 18cm. Cut
left-over gold/silver blocks from the previous
project into 0.5cm strips, emboss them, then stick
to the card as shown in the diagram on page 32.

Referring to the photograph on page 29, weave
a length of gold wire through the mesh (corner to
corner), threading on star beads at regular
intervals. Referring to the instructions on page 6,
make an eyelet at each end of the wire, then curl
the ends round by hand. Make an eyelet on each
end of a 26cm length of wire, then hand wind a
double-ended spiral. Repeat with another 26cm
length of wire. Use 15cm lengths of wire and a
similar technique to make two single-ended spirals,
each with an eyelet on each end. Attach all the
spirals to the mesh by threading their ends through
the mesh.

Position the mesh in the middle of the
checkerboard border, pierce a few holes through
the card, then use gold thread to sew the mesh to
the card. Secure the spirals in place in a similar
manner. Use sticky tape to secure the ends of the
thread to the back of the card.

Trim the A5 card to 12.5 x 16 cm, then use
double-sided sticky tape to stick this to the inside
of the card to cover the stitching.

Large Frame for Mirror or Picture

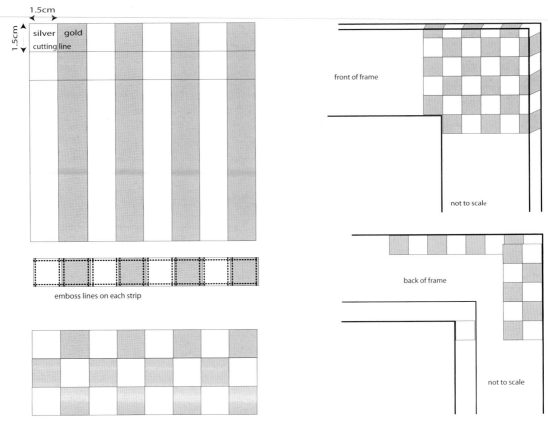

1.5cm

1.5cm

silver | gold
cutting line

emboss lines on each strip

attach strips to corners of frame in a checkerboard pattern

front of frame

not to scale

back of frame

not to scale

Checkerboard Border Card.
Enlarge pattern by 200%

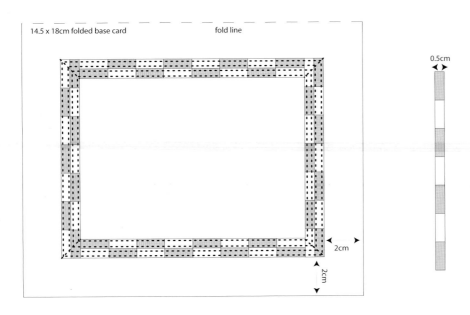

14.5 x 18cm folded base card   fold line

2cm

2cm

0.5cm

PURSES

Jana Ewy, an American colleague gave me the idea of making neck purses; they are original and great fun to make. They can be purely decorative and worn as jewellery, or be functional if, for example, you need somewhere to keep business cards readily available. They make ideal presents for special friends and family. For an extra surprise, slip a small greetings card with a personalized message inside the purse.

SILVER KNITTED PURSE
(see page 33, bottom left)

To add that 'designer' touch to any outfit, attach this delightful silver purse to your belt. If you use a different size of purse frame you will need to count the holes in the top bar of the frame (not the side holes) and cast on the same number of stitches as holes. You may also have to knit more (or less) rows to achieve a balanced appearance.

You will need
- 3mm bamboo (or wooden) knitting needles
- 7cm silver purse frame with chain
- 30SWG silvered wire

Instructions
Cast on 21 stitches using the needle method (the thumb method of casting on does not work with wire). Knit 70 rows, slipping the first stitch of each row instead of knitting it to give neat side edges. Cast off. Fold the knitting in half and lay the purse frame on the knitting, aligning the holes in the top bar of the frame with the cast-on edges. Slot a coloured thread through both edges of the knitting just below the frame hinge. Cut a length of wire and oversew both sides of the knitting, working from the fold to the coloured thread. Use wire to oversew each stitch of the cast-on edge to a hole in the top bar. Oversew the edges of the knitting to the holes at each side of the frame. Carefully push the knitting together so that the stitches become closer together and the knitting fits within the area of the frame.

Tip: To secure the wire at the start of sewing, lay about 1cm of wire along the seam and then oversew to trap the end of the wire. To secure the wire when finishing, make several stitches then weave the end of the wire back through.

NECK PURSE WITH SILVER AND STAMPED TRIM
(see page 33, top right)

You will need
- A4 sheet of dark blue card
- piece of Art Emboss lightweight aluminium
- black permanent ink pad and rubber stamp of your choice
- heat gun and heat-proof craft sheet
- texturing mallet
- two 3mm silver eyelets and eyelet setting tool
- 3mm circle punch
- needle-nosed pliers
- six each of silver eye pins and head pins
- wire winder and smallest mandrel
- 27SWG silver wire
- eight silver coloured square beads
- six transparent or silver coloured rocaille beads
- approximately 75cm of silver coloured cord
- 1cm length of 2cm-wide black self-adhesive, hook-and-loop Velcro
- double-sided sticky tape and sheet

Instructions
Referring to the diagrams opposite, enlarge the pattern by 200% and cut out both pieces of the purse from the dark blue card. Score the fold lines, pierce the holes for the eye pins, punch the eyelet holes, then set the eyelets into the holes.

Cut the three tinted shapes on the pattern from the aluminium, then use black permanent ink and the rubber stamp to create a random pattern on each shape. Working on the heat-proof sheet, dry the ink with the heat gun. Use the mallet to add texture to each shape. Use double-sided sticky sheet to attach the metal shapes on the card purse shapes, then use the lino roller to secure the metal to the card.

Neck Purse with Silver and Stamped Trim. Enlarge pattern by 200%

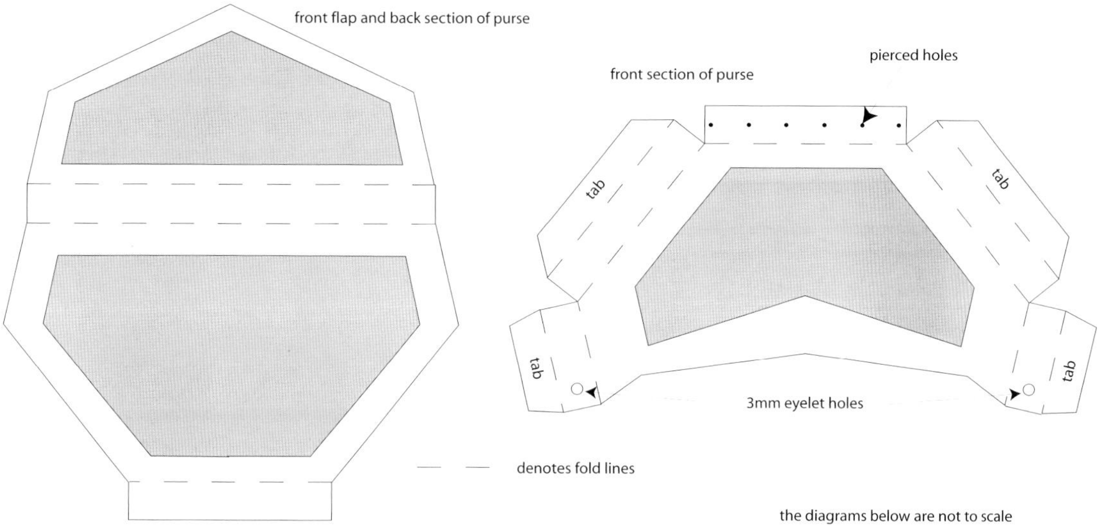

front flap and back section of purse

pierced holes

front section of purse

tab

tab

tab

tab

3mm eyelet holes

– – – – denotes fold lines

the diagrams below are not to scale

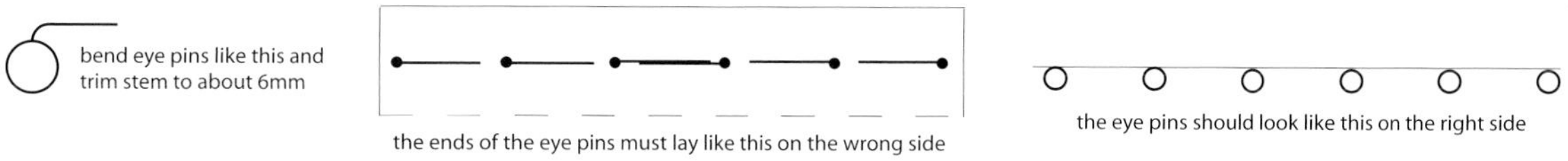

bend eye pins like this and trim stem to about 6mm

the ends of the eye pins must lay like this on the wrong side

the eye pins should look like this on the right side

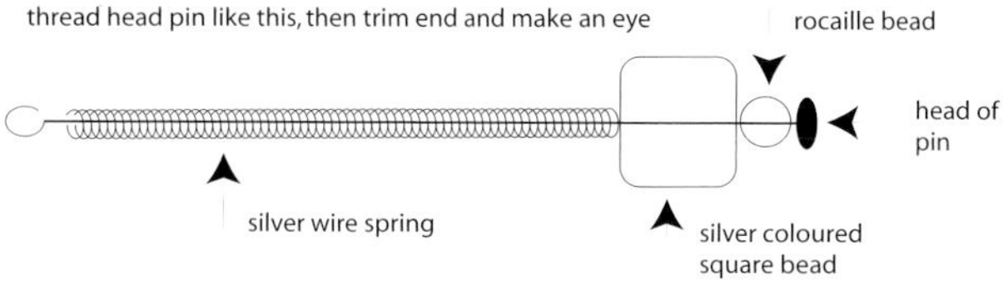

thread head pin like this, then trim end and make an eye

rocaille bead

head of pin

silver wire spring

silver coloured square bead

Referring to the diagram above, use the needle-nosed pliers to bend the stem of the eye pin, then trim the stem to 6mm. Working with the right side of the lower front section of the purse face up, push an eye pin through each of the pierced holes. Turn the piece over and place a strip of double-sided sticky tape across the eye-pin stems to hold them in place. Turn the piece face up and place more strips of tape on the other four tabs.

Fold along the scored lines on both pieces of the purse. Remove the protective paper from the tape over the eye-pin stems, then, with both pieces of the purse face up, stick this tab on top of the bottom of the back section of the purse. Remove the protective paper from the other tabs and stick the tabs to the back section of the purse.

Wind a full mandrel of silver wire, then cut the spring into two 2.5cm, two 3cm and two 3.5cm lengths. Referring to the diagram above, thread a rocaille bead, a square silver bead and a length of spring on each of the six head pins. Trim each stem, make eyes with needle-nose pliers, then attach the head pins to the eye pins on the bottom of the purse; attach the longest ones in the centre and the shortest at each end.

Now add the neck cord. Thread a square silver bead on the end of the silver cord, knot the end of the cord to retain the bead, then pass the other end of the cord through the eyelet (from inside the purse). Pass the cord through the other eyelet (from the outside), thread a bead on the cord and knot the end to complete the neck cord.

Remove the protective paper from one side of the Velcro and stick this under the point of the front flap. Remove the protective paper from the other side of the Velcro, close the front flap and apply pressure to stick the Velcro on the main body of the purse.

COPPER MESH NECK PURSE
(see page 33, bottom right)

You will need
- 11 x 27cm piece of copper wire mesh
- small piece of gold coloured metal
- texturing mallet
- black permanent ink pad and your choice of rubber stamp
- heat gun and heat-proof craft sheet
- large flat gold coloured bead
- small gold coloured bead
- petrol coloured rocaille beads
- 72cm gold coloured cord
- gold thread and a needle
- ruler
- lino roller
- needle tool

- **Optional:** three gold coloured pendant spacers, nine small gold coloured charms and three gold jump rings

Instructions
Enlarge the pattern (right) by 200% and cut the shape from the copper mesh. Score the folds, place the ruler on the scored line and fold in the raw edges of the mesh around the purse, making two folds on the front flap. Use the lino roller to flatten the edges.

Working on the heat-proof sheet, use the heat gun to create a marbled effect on the copper. You may want to try this technique on a scrap piece of copper mesh first.

Fold along the scored line to bring the front up on top of the back. Use the needle tool to pierce holes through all layers on each side of the purse. Referring to the diagram (right), and working from the bottom upwards, oversew with gold thread, adding a rocaille bead on each stitch. Work back down, again adding a bead on each stitch, to end with one row of beads on the front and one on the back. Repeat the process on the other side of the purse.

Pierce the two holes for the neck cord. Cut a 60cm length of gold cord, thread each end through the back of the holes, tie knots to secure the cord and trim off excess.

Copper Mesh Neck Purse
Enlarge pattern by 200%

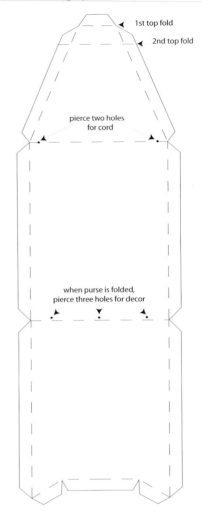

1st top fold
2nd top fold
pierce two holes for cord
when purse is folded, pierce three holes for decor

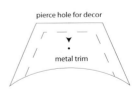

pierce hole for decor
metal trim

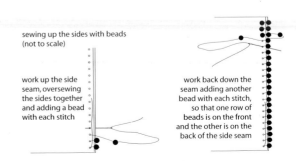

sewing up the sides with beads (not to scale)

work up the side seam, oversewing the sides together and adding a bead with each stitch

work back down the seam adding another bead with each stitch, so that one row of beads is on the front and the other is on the back of the side seam

Referring to the diagram on page 36, cut out the trim from gold coloured metal and score the dashed lines. Use the permanent ink and rubber stamp to create a random pattern on the metal, then dry this with the heat gun on the heat-proof sheet. Fold the three edges along the scored lines, then slide the metal on to the bottom of the front flap.

Pierce a hole through the metal and the top layer of mesh of the front flap (not the double-folded tab). Pass one end of the remaining 12cm of cord through the hole from the back of the flap and thread on the flat gold bead. Thread on the small gold bead, take the cord back though the flat bead and the hole in the metal and mesh. Knot the two ends of the cord together so that the top of the flat gold bead sits 1cm below the hole. Trim off excess cord. Cover the knot with the double-folded tab, then use the lino roller to ensure that all the folded edges are flat.

Pierce three holes through the bottom of the purse, then use jump rings to suspend your chosen pendants or charms.

GOLD METAL EMBOSSED NECK PURSE (see page 33, top left)

You will need
• 12 x 20cm piece of gold coloured metal
• A4 sheet of dark green card
• embossing template of your choice
• approximately 80cm of gold cord
• two 3mm silver eyelets and eyelet setting tool
• 3mm circle punch
• two 5mm gold beads
• embossing tools and foam mat
• 1cm length of 2cm-wide black self-adhesive hook-and-loop Velcro
• double-sided sticky tape and sheet

Instructions
Enlarge the pattern above by 200% and cut out the shape from the green card. Score the fold lines, punch the eyelet holes and set the eyelets in place.

Cut the three tinted shapes from gold coloured metal, then referring to the instructions on page 7, emboss a central design on the front flap. Working on the front of the metal, use a fine ball tool to

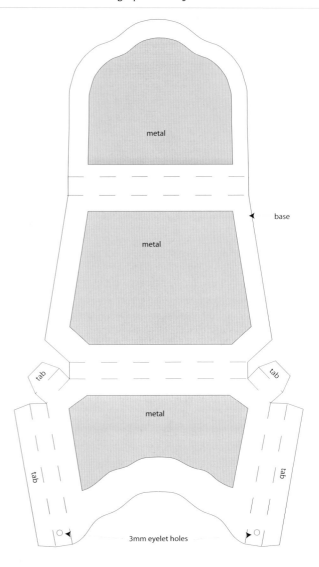

Gold Metal Embossed Neck Purse.
Enlarge pattern by 200%

stipple the areas between the embossing, then stipple a small border round the outside of the design. Use an embossing wheel to create raised dots round the edges of the metal shape. Decorate the other two metal shapes in a similar manner, using the same central motif and two corner designs. Use double-sided sticky sheet to attach all three pieces of metal on the base card, then use a lino roller to secure.

Apply strips of double-sided sticky tape to the tabs on the front section of the purse. Fold all the scored fold lines, then stick the tabs to the back section of the purse.

Now add the neck cord. Thread a square silver bead on the end of the silver cord and knot the end of the cord to retain the bead. Pass the other end of the cord through the eyelet (from inside the purse) and then thread it through the other eyelet (from the outside). Thread a bead on the cord and knot the end to complete the neck cord.

Remove the protective paper from one side of the Velcro and stick this under the point of the front flap. Remove the protective paper from the other side of the Velcro, close the front flap and apply pressure to stick the Velcro on the main body of the purse.

JEWELLERY

COPPER CHOKER WITH PENDANT
(see page 37, middle)

You will need
- 23SWG copper wire
- a small length of 19SWG copper wire
- 30cm length of 12SWG copper wire
- 85cm of 1.2cm wide dark green Paris binding
- 6mm diameter circular mandrel
- 1cm diameter wooden dowel
- rectangular mandrel (1. x 0.3 x 18cm)
- club hammer or small anvil
- medium or heavyweight metal hammer
- fine round file
- insulated pliers and needle-nosed pliers
- side snips
- lino roller
- heat gun

Instructions
Using the rectangular mandrel and 23SWG copper wire, wind a full mandrel. Slide the wound wire off the mandrel and gently pull it, opening it to leave about 2mm between each coil. Hold the spring round your neck, or that of the recipient, and cut it to size. Thread the Paris binding through the coil and lay the work on a smooth, firm surface. Carefully flatten one end of the coil with a finger, then use the lino roller to flatten the whole spring. Check that the Paris binding fits neatly when you tie it round your neck; if necessary, trim off any excess coil. Carefully file the ends of the wire to remove any sharp edges and then tuck them back into the inside of the flattened coil. This ensures that the ends do not scratch the wearer's neck or snag clothing.

Warm the length of 12SWG copper wire with a heat gun, then using the wooden dowel to form smooth shapes, create a pendant. This is the diagram for my pendant, but by all means be creative! File the ends of the wire to remove sharp edges, then use the widest parts of the needle-nosed pliers to form eyelets at each end of the pendant.

This section is optional, but very effective. Working on the floor or a bench (not the kitchen table), set the wire on the largest flat surface of the club hammer (or an anvil if you have one). Holding the wire with insulated pliers, use the heat gun to soften the wire, then hammer it with a medium or heavyweight hammer. Turn the wire over, reheat it, then hammer it again. Continue this process until both sides are flat and even along the length. The finished pendant will have a matte finish.

Wind the 19SWG wire round the 6mm mandrel to make a mini coil. Remove the coil, then use side snips to cut along the length of the coil to make jump rings (you only need one for this project, but you will soon find a use for the others). Locate the middle of the choker and pierce a hole in one edge of the Paris binding. Pass the jump ring through the hole, attach the pendant, then close the jump ring securely.

Pendant for
Copper Choker.
Enlarge by 200%

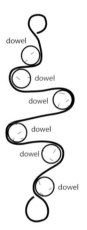

THREE-STRAND GOLD WIRE FRENCH KNITTING NECKLACE
(see page 37, top)

You will need
- 30SWG gold wire
- 6mm diameter red faceted glass beads
- four-pin French knitting bobbin
- needle and crochet hook
- six oval gold beads
- six crimp beads
- two three-strand necklace spacers
- seven-strand nylon-coated bead stringing wire (brass or gold colour)
- three 4mm diameter gold jump rings and one 6mm diameter gold coloured bolt fastener

Instructions
Use the gold wire and the French knitting bobbin to knit three ropes – 60, 70 and 80cm in length – dropping a red bead into the centre of the knitting every 2cm for the 60 and 80cm lengths and every 10cm for the 70cm one. Sew the ends of the wire securely into each end of the ropes.

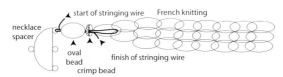

Referring to the diagram above, thread a length of stringing wire through an oval bead and a crimp bead and through the end of one knitted rope. Take the stringing wire back through both beads, over a ring in the necklet spacer, then back through the beads again. Grasp both ends of the stringing wire and pull the beads and French knitting tightly together. Flatten the crimp bead to secure the stringing wire and snip off any excess wire. Repeat this process at the other end of the rope with the second necklet spacer, then add the other two ropes in the same way. Attach a small jump ring to one necklet spacer and attach the bolt fastener to this with another small jump ring. Attach a small jump ring to the other necklet spacer and attach the large jump ring to this to complete the project.

FRIENDLY PLASTIC BROOCH
(see page 37, right)

You will need
- 3.5cm and 1.5cm squares of Friendly Plastic
- 15cm length of 23SWG silver wire
- three flat backed glass faux diamonds
- length of French knitting made with 30SWG dark green wire
- rubber stamp of your choice to texture the Friendly Plastic
- 6cm square of silver coloured metal
- texturing mallet
- 4.5cm square of mount board or thick card
- 4.5cm square of black card
- 3cm long brooch pin
- double-sided sticky sheet
- high-tack glue
- one, 1cm and two 0.5cm dia. silver jump rings
- heat gun
- two flat fancy wire beads

Instructions
Heat both squares of Friendly Plastic and texture them with a rubber stamp. Cut the French knitting into two 4cm, and one 7cm lengths. Referring to the diagram on page 41, reheat the 3.5cm square of plastic and embed the 4cm lengths of knitting across opposite corners, and the 7cm length across the middle, leaving the ends hanging over the sides. Embed the fancy wire beads in the spaces between the knitting. Use high-tack glue to attach two of the flat-backed glass stones to the centre of each fancy bead. Hammer the length of wire evenly on both sides to flatten it slightly (there is no need to heat it), then cut it into two 4cm and one 7cm lengths. Lay these across the centre of each strip of knitting, bend the ends of the knitting and the flattened wire behind the plastic and trim to neaten.

Gently texture the silver coloured metal then cover the wrong side with double-sided sticky sheet. Remove the backing paper, then centre the square of mount board over the metal and press into place. Mitre the metal corners and smooth the flaps down on to the mount board. Use a lino roller on both sides to secure. Neaten the back of the mount board with the square of black card.

Friendly Plastic Brooch. Enlarge pattern by 200%

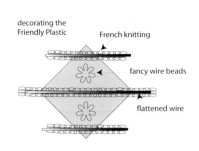

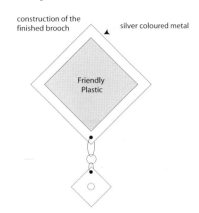

Use double-sided sticky sheet to attach the 3.5cm plastic square to the silver square.

Pierce a small hole through one corner of the metal and the layers beneath, and another through one corner of the small square of plastic. Push the large jump ring through the hole in the silver square and a small jump ring through that in the plastic square. Use another small jump ring to join the two components together. Use high-tack glue to attach the remaining glass stone in the middle of the small square and the brooch pin to the upper half of the large square.

TASSEL BAR WIRE NECKLACE
(see page 37, left)

You will need
- 19 and 23SWG blue wire
- 30 or 33SWG silver wire
- seventeen square silver coloured beads
- wire winder with 2mm circular mandrel
- eighteen jump rings made on a 4mm circular mandrel and one made on a 6mm mandrel
- needle-nosed pliers and side cutters

Instructions
Use the 23SWG blue wire to wind a long coil on a 2mm mandrel, then cut this into eight 3cm lengths. Referring to the diagram (right) use 19SWG blue wire to make each 3cm coil into a bar bead; make an eye at one end of the wire, thread the other end through the coil, cut the wire and make a second eye.

Use either 30 or 33SWG silver wire to wind a long coil on a 2mm mandrel. Cut an 8cm length, then, referring to the photograph on page 37, attach one end of the silver coil to a blue coil bar bead. Wind the silver coil round the blue coil in a spiral form and attach the end to the bar bead. Repeat with another 8cm length of silver coil and a blue coil bar bead.

Use the 19SWG blue wire and a single square silver bead to make six short bar beads. Use the same wire to make eighteen jump rings on a 4mm mandrel and one on a 6mm mandrel.

Use 30 or 33SWG silver wire and the 2mm mandrel to wind several long coils, then cut these coils into eleven lengths: two 2.5cm; two 3cm; two 3.5cm; two 4cm; two 4.5cm and one 5cm.

Tassel Bar Wire Necklace

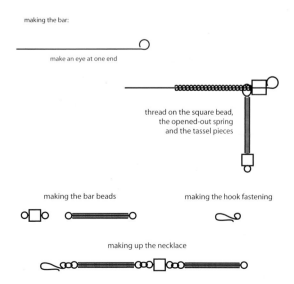

Assemble the tassel pieces in the same way as the bar beads but, this time, make a tiny eye on one end of the wire, thread on a square bead and a coil and then make a larger eye at the other end.

Open out a length of 23SWG blue wire coil to approximately 2.7cm (this is for the tassel bar). Now cut an 8cm length of 19SWG blue wire, make an eye at one end, then thread on a square bead and the opened out blue coil. Assemble the tassels: start with one of the smallest lengths, work up to the largest, then graduate back down to the smallest length. Subject to the size of the eyes on the end of the tassel, you may have to wind the tassels along the opened out blue coil to position them. When all tassels have been assembled, add another square bead and finish the bar with another eye.

Referring to the diagram on page 41, use 19SWG blue wire to make a hook, and file off any sharp edges.

Assemble the necklace. Use small jump rings to connect the hook to a blue wire bar bead, then the wire bar bead to a square silver bar bead. Continue until you have connected the fourth wire bar bead. Connect this to a silver and blue wire bead and then connect one end of the tassel bar. Repeat this process, but in the reverse order, for the other side of the necklace, finishing with the large blue jump ring.

Black Velvet Choker with French Knitting Trim

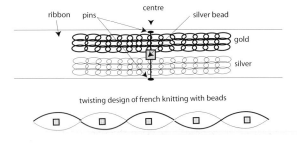

twisting design of french knitting with beads

BLACK VELVET CHOKER WITH FRENCH KNITTING TRIM
(see page 37, bottom)

You will need
- 90cm of 2.4cm wide black velvet ribbon
- two 40cm lengths of French knitting made with 30SWG wire, one gold and one silver
- six square silver beads
- large black and silver drop bead
- two small silver beads
- one silver head pin
- one large silver jump ring made on a 4mm mandrel or a purchased real silver jump ring
- silver and gold fine thread and a needle
- dressmaking pins

Instructions
Place both ends of the ribbon together and cut the ends at an angle to prevent the ribbon from fraying. Use a lino roller to flatten both pieces of French knitting.

Referring to the diagram below left, pin the middle of the length of gold French knitting to the middle of the ribbon, leaving a 0.3cm gap between the top edge of the ribbon and the top of the knitting. Pin the silver knitting in a similar manner, leaving a 0.3cm gap between the bottom of the knitting and the bottom edge of the ribbon.

Working from the centre out to one end, twist the two rows of knitting, passing silver over gold or *vice versa*, then pin each to the ribbon as before. Continue twisting and pinning, then, when the knitting runs out, bring the two ends of knitting together to give a neat finish. Repeat this process from the centre out to the other end. If necessary, adjust the positions of the pins to equalize the twists. Use the gold and silver thread to sew the knitting to the ribbon and to add the square silver beads in the loops.

Thread a small silver bead, the drop bead and another small silver bead on the head pin. Trim the head pin stem and make an eye. Pierce a hole in the centre of the bottom edge of the ribbon, and use the jump ring to attach the pendant to the ribbon. Close the jump ring.

BOOKS

MEMO BLOCK (see page 45, top)

You will need

- two 8cm squares and one 3 x 8cm rectangle of greyboard (or mount board)
- two 8.5 x 2cm strips of linen (or bookbinders' shirting) and bookbinders' glue
- 10 x 26.5cm piece of sapphire coloured metal
- 7cm square of diamond mesh
- 19SWG silver wire
- wire jig
- relief gloss lacquer
- 7.5 x 18.9cm piece of patterned paper
- 7.5 x 18.9cm piece of 100gsm white paper
- Needle tool
- silver thread and needle
- 7.6cm square block of 3M Post-it notes
- double-sided sticky sheet

Instructions

Referring to the diagram above, use bookbinders' glue to adhere the greyboard to the linen to form the carcass of the memo block. Stick pieces of double-sided sticky sheet on to all three pieces of greyboard. Remove the backing paper from one of the squares and centre the whole greyboard carcass on to the sapphire coloured metal. Bend the metal round a spine fold, remove backing sheet from the spine and smooth the metal on to the greyboard. Repeat the process for the second spine fold and the last piece of greyboard. Snip the metal at each end of the spine folds, bend the metal over the edges of the carcass, smooth into place, then use a lino roller to make sharp edges.

Cover a 6cm square in the centre of the outside front cover with a thin coat of relief gloss lacquer. Set the the diamond mesh on the lacquer, then leave to dry thoroughly, preferably overnight.

Memo Block. Enlarge by 200%

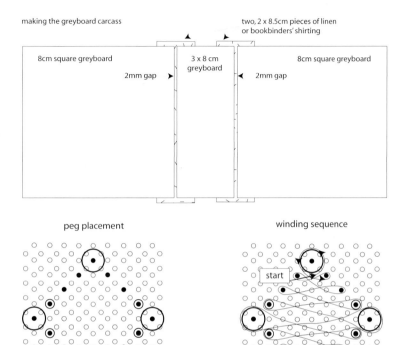

making the greyboard carcass

two, 2 x 8.5cm pieces of linen or bookbinders' shirting

8cm square greyboard

2mm gap

3 x 8 cm greyboard

2mm gap

8cm square greyboard

peg placement

winding sequence

start

finish

○	holes in jig	◉	4mm peg
●	2mm peg	⦿	10mm peg

Referring to the diagrams above, wind the silver wire decoration. Make full circles at each end, then cut off the excess wire. Referring to the instructions on page 6, flatten the shape, then pull it until it measures 8.5cm from top to bottom. Referring to page 45, position the wire shape on the diamond mesh and pierce holes through the cover at each end of the shape. Use silver thread to sew the wire decoration on to the cover.

Glue the patterned paper to the white paper and then glue the white side to the inside of the block to give a neat finish. Finally, attach the Post-it note block.

GOLD HANDBAG NOTEBOOK
(see opposite, left)

You will need
- two 10 x 5.5cm pieces of greyboard
- white paper to make the pages
- two 10 x 5.5cm pieces of gold paper
- two 9.5 x 5cm pieces of gold hologram card
- two 12 x 7.5cm pieces of gold metal mesh
- 5mm hole punch
- double-sided sticky sheet
- gold cord
- charms and beads

Instructions
Round off the corners of both pieces of greyboard and punch a hole as shown in the diagram below. Use the pattern for the greyboard covers to make the white paper pages for your note book and two gold paper pages (the first and last pages of the notebook), then punch holes through these.

Use double-sided sticky sheet to attach the gold metal mesh to one side of both pieces of greyboard then smooth the metal over to the back of the boards. Align the punch again and punch through the metal. Use double-sided sticky sheet to attach the gold hologram card to the inside covers, then punch a hole through the card.

Cut two, three or four 25cm lengths of cord (dependent on the thickness of the cord) to bind the notebook. Fold all the cords in half, pass the loops through the punched holes, then pass the ends through the loops and tighten. This 'knot' expands when the book is opened and can be pulled tight when it is closed. Decorate the cords with colour coordinated lengths of wire coils, beads or charms. I also decorated the cover with flat coin charms and a flat-backed glass stone.

SILVER HANDBAG NOTEBOOK
(see opposite, right)

You will need
- two 10 x 5.5cm pieces of greyboard
- white paper to make the pages
- two 10 x 5.5cm pieces of silver paper
- two 9.5 x 5cm pieces of silver hologram card
- two 12 x 7.5cm pieces of silver coloured metal
- 5mm hole punch
- double-sided sticky sheet
- silver cord
- charms and beads
- embossing tools and foam mat
- Lazertrans or other decal making products

Instructions
Round off the corners of both pieces of greyboard and punch a hole as shown in the diagram below. Use the pattern for the greyboard covers to make the white paper pages for your notebook and two silver paper pages (the first and last pages of the notebook), then punch holes through these.

Make three enlarged photocopies of the head design on the pattern below. Referring to the photograph opposite, cut out two heads, removing the line design around the head, then make two decals. Place the complete image of the third photocopy on the back of one sheet of metal, then emboss just the line design round the head. Repeat this process on the other piece of metal. Stick a head decal between the embossed lines on the front of each piece of metal.

Referring to the instructions for the gold notebook, stick the metal to the covers, assemble the notebook and decorate the cords.

Handbag Notebooks
Enlarge patterns by 200%

two, 10 x 5.5cm greyboard covers

two, 9.5 x 5cm halogram cards (inside covers)

ORIENTAL ALBUM OR NOTEBOOK (see
page 45, bottom)

You will need
- pieces of greyboard cut to the following sizes:
  front cover flap, 15.2 x 15.5cm
  front cover hinge, 3 x 15.5cm
  back cover, 18.5 x 15.5cm
  front cover panel, 14.5 x 14.5cm
- 2 x 16cm piece of linen (or bookbinders' shirting)
- two 23.5 x 20.5 pieces of black linen (or bookbinders' shirting)
- bookbinders' glue
- **Optional:** Bookbinders' press
- four 15 x 18cm pieces of oriental paper

- 16cm square of gold coloured metal
- twelve 36 x 15cm pieces of white paper
- oriental-key, border-type embossing template
- embossing tools and foam mat
- double-sided sticky sheet
- Lazertrans or other decal-making product
- 5cm square oriental design paper or a Chinese Lion Dog tea bag paper for the decal
- 5mm hole punch
- gold cord
- beads and decoration for tassels

Oriental Album. Enlarge patterns by 200%

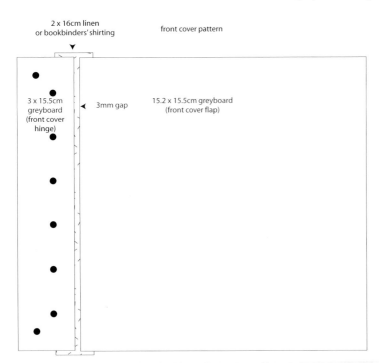

2 x 16cm linen
or bookbinders' shirting

front cover pattern

3 x 15.5cm
greyboard
(front cover
hinge)

3mm gap

15.2 x 15.5cm greyboard
(front cover flap)

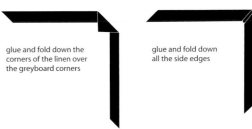

folding down the corners of linen (not to scale)

glue and fold down the
corners of the linen over
the greyboard corners

glue and fold down
all the side edges

Instructions

Referring to the diagram opposite, use bookbinders' glue to adhere the 2 x 16cm piece of linen to the front cover flap and the front cover hinge pieces of greyboard. When the glue is dry, use the pattern as a template to punch the holes in the front cover hinge. Use these holes to make and punch another set for the back cover. Spread bookbinders' glue on the right side of the back cover and hinged front cover boards and centre each of them on the back of the pieces of black bookbinders' linen. Turn the boards over, then glue and fold the corners and sides as shown in the diagram opposite. Interleave the covered board with silicone paper, set some heavy books on top, and leave to dry. If you own a bookbinders' press, all the better.

Punch holes through the linen on both covers. Use bookbinders' glue to attach two of the pieces of oriental paper on the inside of the front and back covers to neaten them. Press until dry, then punch holes through the paper.

Referring to the photograph on page 45, and the diagram below, emboss the design on to the gold coloured metal. Use an embossing wheel to create the two squares of raised dots, a ball tool and a ruler for the outer square and the brass template for the border. Use double-sided sticky sheet to attach the metal in the centre of the remaining square of greyboard, smoothing the outer edges of the metal over on to the back of the board. Make the decal and stick it in the centre of the embossed metal.

Fold the sheets of white paper in half to form 18 x 15cm pages. Stick one piece of oriental paper on the front of one of the folded pages and one one on the back of another. Set aside to dry.

Stack the folded pages on top of each other (with the oriental paper pages at top and bottom of the pile), then hold the stack together with a spring clip. Use the front cover as a guide to punch the holes through all the pages.

Set the pages between the covers and align all the holes. Referring to the diagram on page 48, use Japanese stab binding and gold cord to bind the book. Finish off the end by bringing it round to the front and passing it through the same hole from front to back, then pull the cord tight. Repeat with the other end.

embossing plan for metal front

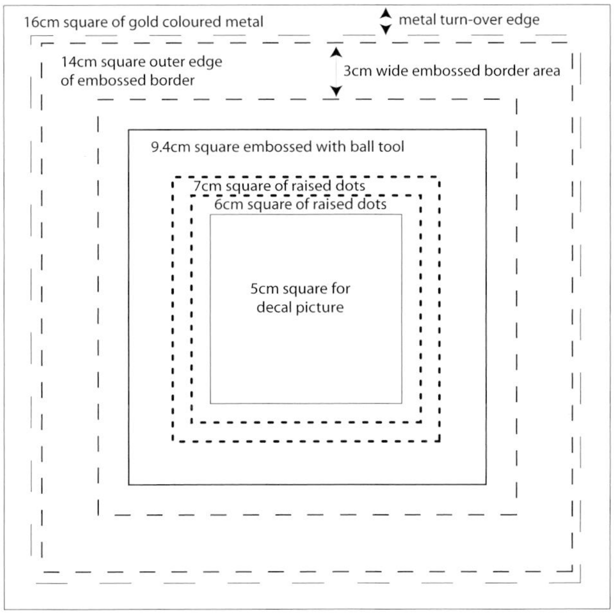

16cm square of gold coloured metal

metal turn-over edge

14cm square outer edge of embossed border

3cm wide embossed border area

9.4cm square embossed with ball tool

7cm square of raised dots

6cm square of raised dots

5cm square for decal picture

Japanese stab binding

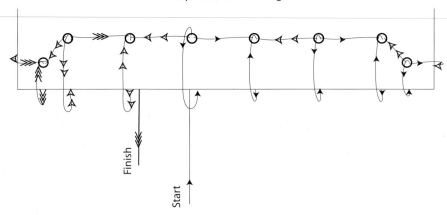

Finish

Start

Cut two 30cm pieces of gold cord. Loop one cord through the double thread on the front of the book near the hole and knot securely. Pass both ends of the cord through a large gold bead, then decorate each cord with beads and gold wire coils Knot the ends, then fray the remaining lengths of cord to complete a tassel. Repeat this procedure with the other length of cord.

Turn the book over and carefully cut off any of the stab binding cord that is left. Do this so that the cut ends are flush to the punched hole.

Tip: For a really professional look, you can make your own matching oriental beads to decorate the cord tassels. Cut 1 x 15cm strips of gold metal. Roll a strip round a skewer tightly to form a barrel bead (use high-tack glue to secure the end of the strip), then decorate the bead by glueing on small pieces of oriental paper.